# Death & Divorce

*Enduring Pain & Processing Grief*
*for God's Divine Purpose*

Daniall Marshall Foskey, LPC, LCMHC

Copyright © 2022 Daniall Marshall Foskey

All rights reserved.

ISBN: 9798366555142
**Imprint:** Independently published

# DEDICATION

To my parents, Daniel and Mary Marshall, whose example of marriage epitomized a union ordained by God: your marriage was the lens I looked through as a child to visualize what I wanted to experience as an adult; and your unconditional love, protectiveness, and support prepared me to be brave enough to walk away from a trying situation and trust that God would turn it into a triumph! Daddy, your prelude towards death was my introduction to living life on purpose. Thank you.

To my brothers, Steven and Andrew Marshall, my siblings whom I see as Superman and Iron Man in the natural world (when you are not irritating me, but I digress): you "fathered" your nephews when their dad was unable to be present and taught me that I did not have to do it all alone. Thank you.

To my sister-in-law, Jennifer Weinstein Marshall: if you weren't a different race, I would forget you weren't blood. The way you love your nephews brought healing to their souls … as well as mine. Thank you!!

To my niece, Carly Marshall, and her aunt, Alyson Weinstein: I strive to become the kind of woman to make you both proud. Carly, I hope that I can give you a double portion of Auntie love since Aly is no longer able to. I always think of her when I get to have "Carly & Auntie time" with you.

To the late William "Bill" Brooks and his widow, Sherry Brooks: you were more than neighbors, you were the helping hands of God. Bill, you told me that as long as you were on this earth, my sons would not have to want for anything. Your death, so closely after my dad's death, was devastating; however, Sherry, in the midst of your own grief, you continued to pour into my sons. Thank you.

To my favorite boss, Grace Hopkins, you gave me a chance and hired me changing my life forever.  Being a school counselor gave me the chance to spend so much time with my children, complete my counseling residency for my license and meet countless people who would impact my life. When you retired, you made sure I accomplished my next goal of becoming a middle school counselor. The day of my interview, I almost canceled because I felt that I was too broken. You allowed me to cry in your arms but, you told me to dry my tears and show the principal the counselor that you raved about. I did just that and transitioned through my transition! Thank you!

Lastly, to my two heartbeats, Jaylen and Jai Foskey: you two are the reasons I fought to save myself, so death and divorce would not steal my purpose. Watching the two of you "become" has been the most rewarding aspect of my life!

I dedicate this book to each of you and thank you for your dedication to me.

# TABLE OF CONTENTS

# ACKNOWLEDGMENTS

*This book is for women in pain, written by a woman
who endured pain but did not have to endure it alone.*

I never would have thought that my graduate school presentation about implementing a community-based program for single mothers would be something I would one day need. I already had a heart for this population, but not due to my experience, because at the time I was happily married. I was drawn to this population because of my lineage. My paternal grandmother, Marguerite Redmond Marshall, became a single mother of 8 kids after my grandfather's sudden death. My maternal grandmother, Mary Lou Ware, was also a single mother, yet they both were able to raise their children to be good citizens who became pillars of their communities both academically and career-wise. During my presentation, I was not talking about women like me, however, this moment is now seen as the prophetic foreshadowing of what I would one day endure and overcome.

The friends that I met in my master's program, the same ladies who were in the room during my presentation, would be the women whose friendships beyond the classroom emulated a therapeutic ointment for the wounds of my soul.

Watching Janice Johnson, LPC's divorce restoration process laid the framework for me. She was the muse that I used most often to begin to paint my portrait of recovery. She and Linda Lewter, LPC were often the therapeutic soundboards I used to implement my training for my own healing journey.

Many other women were additionally instrumental in my healing journey. From my colleagues at Oscar Smith Middle School who shared their journeys or became a buffer for me to go through my healing process and continue to be an effective school counselor, to the sisters of Real Women who gave me a safe space to continue to heal and do so unapologetically!

I had so many prophetic prayer warriors who were instruments of encouragement that God used to shine in my darkness and give me a glimpse of my future. I would not have made it without my dear friend, Prophetess, and author Katrina Rene Jones' divine friendship. She has probably poured into me the most over the past 15 years. Dr. Sheryise Williams would intermittently implement what she'd learned from her doctoral studies and infuse it with the prophetic to encourage me. Susan Shell called me at 6:00 am every morning to pray for me for an entire year and the prophetic intercession of Bathsheba Smithen, Pastor Idella McIntire, Tamara Gregory, and Shandha Louis helped heal the contusions of wounds left from the blunt force trauma of my soul.

I now recognize that I am called to usher women who are anointed in various forms of leadership, down the aisle of their divine purpose, even in the midst of their personal pain. I know this because I had to help others as a school counselor and clinician in private practice while experiencing my own turmoil.

However, I now know that my former pastors being business owners, having a Director of Guidance, like Tonya Edmonds, in the school setting; and being surrounded by entrepreneurial powerhouses like Dr. Jannie Robinson, LCSW, and Sheri Matthews Fayton, LPC, provided the support I needed to produce in the midst of my pain!

Launching Psychological Associates of Greater Hampton Roads, PLLC with my friends and colleagues, would prove to be the springboard into my next season. In this setting, I would be forced to truly heal because growth was inevitable!

Being a very sought-out therapist in VA proved that God saw me as a valuable vessel He could use to walk alongside His chosen women; but God wanted more from me. He used the women in my life to pull the creativity from my soul and put it into action in book form.

With that said, I would not be an author without the influences of the many women I've already named, some of whom are authors, as well as Chesapeake Public Schools pioneers (like Gayle Gilmore and Dr. Corprew Boyd) who encouraged this gift in me years ago.

My best friend of over 30 years, Keionda Sanders, and my childhood friends, Audrey Williams and Cindy Reiner have been reading my unpublished pieces of work since 4th grade, so this has been a long time coming!

Not all women are as fortunate as me to have an experimental and relational knowledge of the importance of friendship, but, since I do, I could not conclude this section without celebrating the women who have always been there, my LIFERS, Tywanda Bloodworth, Naschica Morrison, Tamara Mouzon, Caressa Norman, Regina Robinson, and Stephanie White. Also, my VA Life Tribe, Cynthia Barrington Toye, Pamela Dawkins, Ebone'

Granger, Kiesha Hawkins, Valerie Hunter, Darcell Sessoms, and Michelle Wilson.

Furthermore, the women in my lineage, my mother, my grandmothers, my aunts, and my two special Aunties (my daddy's sisters), Margaret Ann Wesson and Martha Teague have all been a part of my becoming.

I've always recognized that my female cousins, The Marshall, Redmond, Smith, and Ware girls: came from greatness, embodied greatness, and exuded greatness. Thus, seeing the greatness in them helped me visualize the greatness in me.

Lastly, Dr. Miracle Pettenger is indeed a miracle worker. I thank her for her patience and wisdom. I am now a published author because God sent her to me.

# FOREWARD

I met Daniall at Regent University in 2003. We were both embarking upon a graduate degree in Community Counseling. When we first met, I immediately encountered her inquisitive, intelligent, and persistent spirit. She asked a million questions and would never settle for being ignored or marginalized by any of our professors. I found this to be annoying, amusing, and admirable all at the same time. We quickly became friends   Little did I know that this young, brilliant, and beautiful soul was listening and comforting me as I was in the midst of my own grief journey. The loss of a marriage that had stood the test of time for twenty-eight years.

As I read her book, *Death and Divorce, Enduring Pain & Processing Grief for God's Divine Purpose!* I am overwhelmed with her unique ability to refuse to edit out the rawness of her pain as she endeavors to help others through their journey. This book captivates the reality of loss and the triumph that can emerge as Daniall admonishes you to **B.R.E.A.T.H.E.** your way to victory.

This is not a book to just make you hopeful … it is also one that will inspire you to become victorious with the comfort, support and guidance of great friends and an All-Knowing God. Daniall's courageous transparency in sharing her testimony is indeed a gust of fresh air to all who read and listen. As a trained trauma specialist, we are taught to encourage others to deal with their grief and trauma at the right time, in the right place and with the right support.  This book is an exemplary resource to have at your side when you're ready to do what Daniall has admonished us to do – **B.R.E.A.T.H.E.!**

*~ Janice R. Johnson, LPC*

# INTRODUCTION

Why did you purchase this book? Take a moment to pause and think. Answer this question from the essence of your soul. I believe you bought this book for one of two reasons. One, you know me and have had a glimpse of my story and want to know more about what happened. Maybe you are interested in how I got through such chaotic experiences. Or two, you know that I am a therapist, and you are looking for a book with substance and some form of expertise to help you get through the most tumultuous storm of your life. Despite your reason, I am glad you and I are here together today. I am so happy that you decided to finally become free from the thing that has caused you to grieve an immensely indescribable form of death – the death of a relationship.

*#youwillpraisehimforyourpain*

My PAIN POSTURED me for PRAYER.

My PRAYERS POSITIONED me in GOD's PRESENCE.

GOD's PRESENCE PREPARED me for my PURPOSE.

My PURPOSE PROPELLED me towards GOD's PLANS.

GOD's PLANS PRECLUDES the perpetuation of
the enemy's plots to destroy my life!

The PRECLUSION of the enemy's plots is
the PRELUDE to GOD's PROMISES ...

And GOD's PROMISES PROMPTS the PRAISE
for my PAST PAIN!!!

# THE POSTURE OF PRAYER & PAIN

What exactly is the prayer posture anyway?  Some may kneel while others lie prostrate, but I found the fetal position most apropos.  I'll never forget the moment I curled myself in a ball and cried out to God.  I lay on my bedroom floor while my sons played outside with their friends.  I'd always loved hearing the echoes of laughter from the neighborhood boys in our cul-de-sac.  My house was where many of the neighborhood kids frequented.  We had a basketball hoop, endless bottles of water, and a safe place where the kids could play void of oncoming traffic.  Some days, the bounce of the ball or the crescendo of competition screams lured me to the window to watch my sons enjoy the ideal life their dad, and I had worked so hard to give them.  That day, their sounds of play did much more than draw me to peek from the spectator's window.  This time it assured me that it was safe for me to curl up tighter and cry.  Heck, who am I kidding?  I wailed!

I longed for the loving hands of my husband to caress me back from reality.  I craved to hear apologetic words of remorse followed by restorative actions.  But instead, I lay nestled on the hard floor of my bedroom, begging God to send my husband home and take away the pain he had inflicted in the depths of my soul.

I cried for what seemed like hours, waiting in vain for my husband to come home and resuscitate my heart from cardiac arrest.  I at least hoped he would take care of the kids so I could just be left alone in my pain.   But he needed to breathe! He needed to get away from me to have the audacity to tell his secret.  I begged him not to leave me alone to sort through the pile of pain, but he just couldn't take what I did.  Was he serious? He couldn't take the fact that I'd confided in people he'd previously deemed he trusted me to vent to.  I explained to him that I only told people I knew could hear our story of betrayal and pray for us.  He didn't care.  He said the guilt and shame were too unbearable.  If he couldn't bear the pain of his self-imposed shame, imagine how agonizing it was for me to try and figure out how to get from underneath the boulder he dropped upon my heart.  I didn't want to betray his trust.  I didn't want to make him "look bad" to people.  I just wanted to learn how to breathe In my suffocating reality.  He didn't come home that night, nor would he answer his phone.

Night fell, and I mustered up the strength to feed my boys and watch our nightly movie.  But I was not present.

*It's during the still, quiet darkness of the hour that*
*life screams the loudest.  The mind races at the*
*speed of Thought once everyone gets still.*
*Be it a flight of ideas or ideas in flight,*
*Thought's destination is unclear as she runs all over*
*the place! You'd think she'd tired, but the still and*
*the dark energize her even the more ...*

*She must be tamed, mustn't she?*
*Daylight's harness tightens its grip via daily*
*demands while Thought fidgets to be set free.*
*But she must oblige because that's just the way it is,*
*but should it be?*

*Even the Bible deems that as a man thinketh,*
*so is he (or she).  Thus, Thoughts will take you by*
*the hands and run with you down the path towards*
*nowhere unless YOU decide there is somewhere*
*else Thought needs to be.*

*Alas, the road less traveled is far ahead.*
*After all, it's during the still, quiet darkness of the*
*hour that life screams the loudest, and minds race*
*at the speed of Thought once everyone gets still.*

*But, now Thought knows exactly where she will go.*
*THERE!  Wherever God leads.*

## I'm Not OK. I Need Help Too!

I was not yet, operating at full capacity; I operated in full capacity. Nothing changed about our routine, but EVERYTHING had changed. Everything remained the same outwardly, but inwardly, I was dying.

I couldn't fathom how my husband could carry on as if he hadn't pulled the very foundation of our marriage from under me and refused to help me regain my footing.

It's one thing to have had an affair but quite another to have one with someone who lived less than 300 feet away. I called her my friend. I prayed for her while she preyed on me. And because of my love for her children, I couldn't bring myself to initiate their collateral damage caused by their mom and my husband. So, I sucked it up, and albeit I confronted her, I never exposed her secret to her husband. I endured for as long as I could. As I write my story, the painful memories escape me as I can no longer detail the timeline of events chronologically. However, I recall that both my husband and neighbor had the audacity to keep up appearances in front of the kids and everyone else, corroborating their narrative with endless carpools and neighborly gestures. But I wasn't having it. It was not enough that my husband willingly let me drag him to pastoral and mental health counselors. Or that he even agreed to sign up for a group at our church for men who had affairs or suffered from sexual addictions. I needed him to consider my feelings and stay clear from his paramour! He couldn't, or he wouldn't. He deemed it because our kids were so close. We did not want to make the kids pay for grown-up mistakes. I understood where he was coming from, but I don't think he understood the depths of my hurt.

My hurt transcended the sting of betrayal.  It was much deeper than the surface layer of discovering the lie.  I was hurt from uncovering the truth!  The truth was that my husband of over 15 years was incapable of loving me like Christ loved the church and was unwilling to give himself for it!  My truth was that I couldn't take the continued rejection and severe disconnection that resulted in the betrayal's unveiling.  I tried to help my husband work through his shame and guilt but sitting before therapists and pastors, session after session was futile.  As hindsight becomes insight, my motive for hurriedly ushering him towards healing was so that he'd become well enough to help me!

## The Fight

So, I fought.  I put on my marital boxing gloves and punched anything that came my way!  Depression, anxiety, mistrust, you name it, and I fought it.  But I was NOT going to give up on my marriage!  I hit Satan with a right uppercut so hard when I allowed my husband to return home and vowed to do all I could to make this marriage work.  But I grew tired.  I was exhausted from all the bobbing and weaving the constant lies my husband spewed to maintain a semblance of control. At the same time, I continued to lose my footing and got knocked down.

**Right Jab:** My husband continued communication  with his paramour deeming our kids should not have to suffer because of what they'd done.  However, he never fully admitted to me what he had actually done.  **Left Jab!**

**Right Hook:** My husband orchestrated it for my son and her son to attend driving school together and didn't consult with me. **Left Hook!**

He just didn't get it.  He didn't understand, or perhaps he didn't care, that their facade of normal neighborly individuals was injuring me!  I did not want that woman around my children! I didn't even want my kids around her kids!

**Right Uppercut:** What nearly took me out was being notified that my husband allowed this woman to check my son out of school early for driving lessons.  I WAS DONE!  I went to her house that moment and didn't care who heard what I said.  The explicit details of that conversation are unnecessary to convey my message, but let's just say I'd finally set a boundary that my sons were off-limits.

My husband confronted me because "her daughter heard everything." I saw a disdain in his eyes that I'd never seen before. Was he furious because a child had been privy to my confrontation, or was he angry because I had forced his paramour's hand?  She finally stopped parading my children around like June Cleaver in a carpool.  I don't know for sure, but both scenarios broke me!  How could he show any regard for her and her family and so little for his own?  At what point was he going to do all he could to make me feel better?  **Left Uppercut!**

## The Final Exam

My husband was driving me insane.  I felt like I was starring in the movie Gaslight, unbeknownst to me. Was he trying to make me think I was crazy?  I certainly felt crazy.  I didn't know all the details of his torrid affair, so I laid on an examination table to get tested for STDs.  I was told countless stories that became a cornucopia for my delirium.  I didn't know what to believe.

   a) He'd had an emotional relationship with our neighbor that had recently become physical
   b) He'd actually had physical relations with her more than

once. Still, it recently started and was over before I discovered it because they didn't want to hurt me.

c) He didn't love her, just me, *except he loved both of us.*
d) He'd also slept with prostitutes about 4 times, *but he really didn't. He just told me that, so I'd back off the neighbor.*
e) He had a porn addiction, *but he didn't have a porn addiction.*
f) He had an affair with one of his employees, *but the affair was not with an employee; it was with a colleague.*

As every lie he told spilled out of my thoughts, it left a pile of mess for me to sort through. So, I finally chose an answer ... *g) ALL OF THE ABOVE.*

It did not matter if we were in a pastoral counselor or a marriage therapist setting. He refused to disclose the truth! Later, he revealed that he could not bear to see the pain in my eyes. But I was far less concerned about the pain seen in my eyes because the pain in my soul was unbearable. So, we were at an impasse. The pastoral counselor became increasingly frustrated because he held on to the biblical principle of the truth setting one free. The first marriage counselor seemed so intimidated by my husband's demeanor that he did not even perform the assessments I had requested to help identify the underlying mental condition. There must have been something present for a person who vowed to love you, to hurt you so bad as my husband did.

So, I fought differently. We decided to do individual counseling and continue going to Falling Forward group sessions facilitated by a leader in our church who had overcome sexual addiction. The men met one night and the women another. It was very helpful to know that other couples who professed to be Christians were experiencing this too. I was not alone. However, as the weeks continued, I sat before women who disclosed that their husbands had relapsed again and again; I could not understand why the group members were turning a blind eye to the blatant disrespect and blaming the devil. I understood that Satan was the catalyst behind all sin and believed in God's grace. However, I was also realistic and recognized that true repentance had to produce change. I discontinued going to the group. I felt that being around women who seemed to use Christianity as a rationale to remain in a position to be sucker punched was causing me more harm. I did not know what to do. I was thankful that my husband "said" he wanted to work on our marriage but recognized that he didn't want to do the very hard part of that work. Instead, he just wanted me to get over it and get back to normal. I just could not "act" normal, so I stood in the fighter's stance, awaiting my opponent's next move.

## The Final Scores

Imagine being me for a moment, if you will. Imagine trying desperately to prove that you were a strong enough Christian to endure the "season of worse" in your marriage before it got better. Imagine sorting through all the lies and trying to decipher the truth. I couldn't do it anymore. I could not allow him to drive me crazy. I still felt like I still had a fight in me, but I couldn't continue to aimlessly swing at everything in my way because I had no idea of what or who was swinging back at me!

We didn't make it, we vowed to fight for our marriage, and I was ready to take on my opponent like Muhammad Ali in his prime! However, even the champ is not considered a champ if he has no one to fight. I was fighting Satan and my husband too. We were not on the same page mentally or spiritually and began to operate more like enemies than teammates. I finally conceded. I took off my boxing gloves and began to train for the biggest fight of my life ... Death VS. Divorce.

# THE PROCESS OF GRIEF

I don't know which is worse, death or divorce. But I can certainly tell you that divorce feels a lot like death. Although theorist Kübler-Ross coined the Stages of Grief to coincide with the process of what the deceased's loved ones would experience, these stages could easily be juxtaposed with the "death" of divorce.

## Denial & Isolation

This stage of grief is perhaps the most tolerable when one is trying to withstand the devastating blows of loss. Being swaddled in the clothes of *Denial* keeps us comforted before being unraveled by the truth. This revealing action forces us into shock, and our feet hit our new reality's cold, hard floors. *Denial* befriended me when I was awakened by the Holy Spirit just moments after my dad's ascension to glory.

Something touched me. It wasn't a touch in the physical sense that we experience in our flesh. It was a touch in my soul. I woke up at 2:45 AM in the morning and sensed that I was the one chosen to usher my family down the aisle of grief. Thus, I put on my crisp white gloves in the spirit and checked on my dad. I had to fight the dichotic fight within my flesh that felt a pseudo sense of comfort as I heard the inhaling of the apparatus that made it appear that my daddy still had breath in his lungs. But something in my soul knew, and I spent a few moments talking to my daddy before church doors of grief flung open.

*Denial* helped me touch him, kiss him, and smile at him, knowing that he was with Jesus. *Denial* helped me conjure up the strength to awaken my mom and deem "daddy's gone." *Denial* was present when my mom and brothers changed my daddy's pajamas, so he'd be nice and clean once the hospice nurse and morticians received his body. *Denial* was my shield of protection as I began to send text messages and make phone calls about my daddy's passing. It calmed my nerves when I couldn't get in touch with my husband, who was SUPPOSED to be with our son Jaylen, who had decided to head back to Virginia to take his end-of-year exam for 10th grade Honors English.

*Denial* insisted that I call my husband before anyone else because that is what I would have done had things been different. *Denial* coerced me to keep calling his cell phone and work phone because eventually, he would recognize it was an emergency, and he'd have to answer. *Denial* coaxed me into fantasizing that my husband's love for me would cause him to put this foolishness aside and run to my rescue! My husband didn't respond to my phone calls for hours. Unfortunately, I had no choice but to tell my son because his dad was not even home. Instead of my son being comforted by a parent when he heard of his PauPau's passing, he sat alone on his bed. At the same time, *Denial* gave him the mental dexterity to head to school and take his exam. *Denial* helped my son ignore that his father had stayed out all night and failed to tell him he was doing so. It enabled him to walk past his weeping father, who cried with his face in his hands with shame because he had not been there. *Finally, Denial* put him on the school bus, and my son began his day as if it were any ordinary day. **Denial** does its best to get grievers through the initial shock, but its temporary buffer soon wears off, and grievers are forced to feel the pain.

As hindsight becomes insight, I now recognize that *Denial* coached me when I was in the boxing ring fighting for my marriage! It helped me withstand the blows of betrayal's deadly punch and keep getting back up before a TKO, total knockout. However, *Denial* can only stay long enough for us to get a grip and secure our footing as we trek down the rocky roads of pain.

## Anger

I often deemed the *Anger* stage of grief as analogous to that of one being nestled in the comforts of their bed and then being startled by the screeching sounds of their alarm clock. Angered by the disrupted state of Rem, the nestled sleeper awakens long enough to hit the snooze button! I was surprised at how well I took my father's passing. Then I became angry!

I was mad at the hospital staff for failing to fully explain that hospice was nothing but a means to help your loved one die without prolonging the inevitable. We may have gone another route had we fully known all the end-of-life plans.

I was angry at my dad's oncologist for asserting that he had stage 2 or 3 lung cancer but would be treating him as if it were stage 4.

I was mad at my dad for not saying he was dying if he had a notion that this would be his final days! I was ticked off at my husband for not allowing me the grace to spend more time with my daddy instead of monopolizing my time fighting with him!

I was mad at my friends who were  there for a season but drifted back to normalcy while my entire life seemed unlovable!

I was mad at my mom for being so stuck in her grief and not strong enough to help me filter through my immense pain!

I was mad at my husband for failing to be there for me, like I was there for him when his grandmother passed away!

And MOST of all, I WAS MAD AT GOD!!!  God failed my family and me!  He watched me lay hands on my daddy for three days and exercise an enormous amount of faith as I declared and decreed that death would NOT be my daddy's portion.  I was mad at all the "prophets" who postulated all that God had in store for my daddy yet, failed to mention that he would not be here to see his legacy unfold!  I was mad that God allowed me to go through a divorce while my daddy was dying and transitioned into a demanding job.

I ebbed and flowed through the stages of grief cyclically but found myself stuck in *Anger* for far too long.

My Christian counterparts weren't comfortable with my grief. They tried to spiritualize my feelings and dismiss my anger by reciting God's Word.  I didn't want to hear God's Word.  God's Word seemed contradictory to me.  After all, He HATED the very thing that I was in the midst of .... **DIVORCE!**

His Word promised me that He'd never leave me or forsake me.  Still, I felt forsaken every time I walked outside and saw my home in foreclosure. Yet, at the same time, the lady who was 50% responsible for destroying my children's lives continued to live her life intact.

*Anger* had taken up residence in my psyche, and I am sad to say it has never been evicted. Albeit I don't walk around displaying anger, it seems to be my go-to emotion when someone hurts me. Grief changed me. It made me remove my rose-colored glasses and see people as who they were instead of who they professed to be.

*Anger* became my go-to trauma response. *Anger* protected my heart from being hurt while at the same time injuring it at its core!

## Bargaining

If *Denial* is the most tolerable of grief's stages, I postulate that *Bargaining* is the least beneficial as it relates to how it helps us navigate our feelings.

In this stage, a griever feels the most vulnerable and, in my opinion, most likely associated with guilt. The griever is tormented by intrusive thoughts of "WHAT IF ..." and "I SHOULD'VE ..."

I felt I should've known my dad was dying because God kept trying to tell me! I should have called my dad more often, but I blamed my new job for my disconnect. In reality, I disconnected from my parents because I didn't want my dad to worry about my sons and me when he could no longer physically run to my rescue. I should have suggested we take my dad to the Cancer Treatment Centers of America, or we should have at least made him adopt a more holistic diet. When he was in his last stages, I pondered If we should have avoided giving him morphine which seemed to take him out with one blow. ***POW!***

*Bargaining* made me question everything. Had I been the cause of my reconciliation not working? Should I have just shut up and pretended not to be hurt instead of being so combative? Why couldn't I just deal with it like other women I'd seen? Why would I allow my kids to grieve their grandpa's death at the same time as their parent's marriage? I'd conceded and stopped fighting for my marriage but *Bargaining* threw punches that I didn't see coming. *Bargaining* had me question whether God was my new opponent. I know that sounds ridiculous coming from a Christian, but this was my thought process for a short time. Did God really love me? Did I do something wrong? I must have done something wrong because all hell was breaking loose in my life. Why would God allow me to be punished this way for no reason?

I dizzied myself from all the bobbing and weaving from *Bargaining's* thoughts, wondering if I ever feel stable again. And just like that, while in the thick of my own grief, I had three 6th-grade students lose a parent within days of each other. I was faced with the difficult decision of whether to run a grief group to help them process their grief journey. I remember sliding down the wall and sitting on the floor when I was informed that another one of my six grade students had lost a parent. I remember the guidance secretary telling me that God must be testing me. I became angry at God all over again. But I decided to help three 11-year-old children do what my 40-year-old self just could not do; to work through the stages of grief and finally live in acceptance but, first, depression.

## Depression

When we think about the stages of grief, the *Depression* stage seems to be the most understood because it is usually the easiest of the stages to recognize. However, just as one's way of grieving is their own, so is one's experience with depression. I did a great job containing my depression for the most part.

First, I'd place my depression in my imaginary container and get through my day as usual, just as I learned in school. Then, I would open my imaginary container at the appropriate time, let my depression out, and feel sad. I told myself that this method of grief worked. However, if I'm being honest, my depression would always jump out of my imaginary container and morph into another stage like a transformer.

Who was I kidding? I was too depressed to deal with three depressed kids and didn't have the wherewithal to plan or organize the grief group! The first group was a mess. I sat in the facilitator's chair in my school's lunch bunch room and cried in front of these kids. I was honest with them about my dad. As fate would have it, one of my students, who was wise beyond her years, said, *"perhaps you were also meant to be a participant in the group and not just a facilitator."* So, alas, I began to wear two hats. I planned the groups, and I participated in every activity. I allowed myself to feel what I was feeling both about my dad's death and my divorce.

I had so many things going on that I often didn't really "feel" depressed. However, I had a depressive life and had to recognize that the symptomology for depression transcended the shedding of tears. For me, depression was not being able to keep my house in order like I once did. It was cooking less and eating out more. Depression was being unorganized and feeling like I was walking on cobblestones. Depression was dreading going to church and seeing the other families remain intact while my family had been ripped apart. Depression was so hard for me. It was the act of allowing myself to let go of the anger and feel the deep sadness of the loss. I was sad that my sons would not be able to go to their childhood home like I still get to do today. I was sad that my future grandkids would not have the chance to experience life with their grandparents being married. I was sad that I wouldn't have a testimony about how God restored my marriage because of my faith and my fight. I was depressed about everything I thought I would get to do with my husband after our kids were grown.  Instead, I had to experience the pain of my loss and allow myself the chance to grieve.

I gave myself permission to let some things fall by the wayside while I set my intentions on the things, I could not lose control over.  Giving myself room to feel made room for me to heal and help walk my students along their healing journey.

## Acceptance

*Acceptance* transcends more than just coming to terms with the fact that your loved one is gone.  It is the essence of being present in life and living your life with purpose, on purpose, and for purpose.  Even though you must do it without your loved one, who has gone home to be with the Lord.

Acceptance is settling into your "new normal" and trusting that God's plans for you are good, even though the current situation doesn't feel good!

And finally, acceptance is surrendering your heart to the Master so that He may align it with the desire to take Him at His Word.  God knows you are hurt, and He promises to send His Comforter.  Therefore, acceptance is also trusting God's plans and being faithful while waiting in the process.

I had longed for the day when I could ascertain that I was experiencing acceptance.  Now that I have and am, I recognize that this stage does not necessarily mean you will exude joy and happiness at every moment of the day.  For myself, it has meant that I have come to a place where I have created a milieu, or atmosphere, conducive for acceptance to manifest.  I still miss my dad immensely.  However, pain is no longer associated with missing him.

Furthermore, as a divorcee, I no longer feel angry that my ex-husband left my children and me in dire straits when he decided he no longer wanted to be a husband or full-time father. I had stewed in anger so long that it became a mantra for my life that I no longer felt served me. So, I forgave the unforgivable and decided to trust God despite what my husband had put me through. I learned to accept that my marriage did not work and that my kids would no longer live the kind of life that I planned for them to live. I accepted that I was a single parent and could no longer do the things for my kids that I was once able to do with two incomes. It was not easy to get to this place of acceptance. In fact, it was the most challenging thing I've ever done. Embracing acceptance meant I had to let go of my bitterness and anger towards my ex-husband and my desire to see him pay for his sins. As long as I was focused on what I had lost, I didn't allow room for God to prove His words to me.

*Acceptance* yielded my will to the will of God and allowed God to do miraculous works in my life! I don't know which is worse, death or divorce, but divorce does feel like death, which we all will experience at some point in our lifetimes.

*Death does NOT stop us from*

*experiencing our loved ones.*

*It simply changes HOW we experience them now.*

*As I walk alongside you through this PROCESS –*

*It is my hope that TOGETHER we discover the way*

*for you to continue to experience your love*

*(albeit differently) in a manner that allows you*

*to FULLY acknowledge your current pain;*

*while at the same time acquiescing to your God –*

*given right to heal from the pain you feel and move*

*forward even in the midst of their absence!*

*~ Daniall Marshall Foskey*

# PRACTICING GOD'S PURPOSE
# IN PRACTICAL WAYS

I can't recall the moment I realized that I could no longer rely on my soon-to-be ex-husband to help me raise our kids. Still, I remember making a conscious decision to release him from being obliged to succumb to my  perception of what his fatherly duties entailed.  For example,  I no longer asked him to help me with any means of transporting the kids.  He had made so many empty promises that resulted in arguments that I found myself reverting to a state of anger.  So, I set boundaries.

I looked in the mirror and saw the reflections of my current reality.  The truth was that my ex-husband decided to walk away and became angry when I obliged.  We were no longer in the ring fighting to save our marriage.  Now, he was an opponent seemingly fighting to win the title belt to ensure my misery. The man I once adored and thought loved me became so angry with me that he intentionally caused unnecessary suffering. By this point, I had settled into the position that purpose had to come from my pain.  So, I took a long glare in Reality's mirror and stared at my truth.  The truth was that, for whatever reason, my ex-husband was more preoccupied with seeing me in torment and agony than shielding our sons from their pain. I faced each reality and fought to trust God no matter what. I finally surrendered to the fact that my husband would not promptly transfer the house's deed to me so I could try to save it.  Therefore, I defaulted on the loan, gave the bank the keys, and proceeded with foreclosure.  The truth was he was not going to pay more money than was mandated by the state, and if I didn't put him on child support, he'd pay when he felt like it.  The truth was the extended family I was once securely a part of had chosen sides, and they did not choose mine!  The truth was my sons would no longer have two parents rooting for them at their sporting events or scholastic awards ceremonies, and I would be 100% responsible for everything from their academic dexterity to their emotional prowess!  This was a tough pill to swallow, but I tilted my head back and swallowed, allowing the truth as I now knew it to dissolve into my new normal.

It was so hard doing the job of two parents all by myself. It was devastating watching my sons suffer in silence. It was especially tough while working a demanding job where I couldn't make ends meet, so I decided I had to make more money. I desperately tried to find a job in my field.  I was a school counselor and had recently obtained my license to practice therapy, so I put my resume out there to no avail.

> *And we know that God causes everything to work*
> *together for the good of those who love God and are*
> *called according to his purpose for them.*
>
> *Romans 8:28 New Living Translation*

So, with tears in my eyes and no idea how I would make it as a single mom, I stood firmly on this scripture and tested God at His Word.  My life had changed so drastically that I could  no lager run to my daddy to rescue me because he was deceased. My mom was still stuck in her grief that I didn't dare bother her, so I suffered in silence and continued to seek God's face.

My sons and I were enduring a desperate season.  While my home was foreclosing, the transmission in my truck went out at the same time as the motor in my son's car. There were so many catastrophic things going on in my life that I'd have to write another chapter just to tell it all; however, I will say that all hell had broken loose, and I felt like I was in a pressure cooker. The awesome thing about a pressure cooker is that it produces results quickly. However, the pressure cooker also requires excessive steam for the outcome to be effective. God had allowed my life to be engulfed with pressure. So much so there were times I felt I could no longer catch my breath. I assume this is how the three Hebrew boys felt in the fiery furnace. I'm sure the temperature became so intense that they could barely breathe. Yet, they did not burn in that furnace because God sent an angel to rescue them, and He did the same for me.

God sent my friend, Janice, to remind me that I had a license to practice therapy and that I didn't need anyone to give me a job when I had the ability to create one myself! I soon began to take the necessary steps to obtain my insurance panels credentials. I rented Janice's office on days she was not using it and became a part-time clinician. For two years, I worked two jobs, and soon, I made the same amount of money working 12 hours a week as a part-time clinician as I did, working 36+ hours at my full-time job. Thus, I made a very difficult decision to walk away from job security and walk into my divine purpose! I have been operating my business full-time for two years as a private practice clinician, and God has been so faithful! I make more money now than I've ever made in my life! And as God would have it, I netted more money alone than my ex-husband and I had done combined! Divorce caused a decrease in my income, and desperation caused me to dig in for my increase!

## *Pause To B.R.E.A.T.H.E.*

My biggest mistake was paying closer attention to everyone else around me while neglecting to pay attention to myself. Women, especially mothers, are guilty of this. On any flight I've ever been on, before taking off, the Flight Attendant always reminds the passengers with kids to put their oxygen masks on before they do their children. Doing this ensures that the adult remains alive and thus is able to assist their child during a crisis. I may not have been on a physical flight, but metaphorically speaking, I'd taken off on life's flight and failed to put on my mask before I ensured my sons wouldn't suffocate. As a therapist, I have created an acronym to remind my clients to BREATHE when in a storm.

*#breathwork*

*GIRL, B.R.E.A.T.H.E. – YOU GOT THIS!*

*I know your current situation has knocked
the wind out of you.*

*I know your circumstances are suffocating,
and it seems as if life keeps tightening its grip
around your airways every time
you think you will be let up for air!*

*I know life's grip seems stronger than your will to fight,
and sometimes you want to give in to asphyxiation,
but I am here to remind you that you have to
B.R.E.A.T.H.E.!*

You have to take your life by the throat and
choke it until it begs YOU for mercy!

Don't let what life has done to you keep you from
inhaling the lessons of pain or exhaling your purpose!

Sis, you have to B.R.E.A.T.H.E.!

- BOW before Him.

- REACH out for help.

- ESTABLISH A LIFE STRATEGY.

- ACCEPT the call on your life.

- THINK positively.

- HAVE FUN!

- EMBRACE your new normal!

It's time to do the BREATHWORK!

## *BOW BEFORE HIM*

*So the people believed; and when they heard that
the Lord had visited the children of Israel and that
He had looked on their affliction, then they bowed
their heads and worshiped.*

*Exodus 4:31 New King James Version*

Whether grieving the loss of a relationship through death or divorce, one must recognize the extent of their vulnerability. When your heart and soul are dealing with immense pain, it is easy to feel alone and think God is not with you. However, during life's most suffocating moments, it is imperative to remember that God is the breath of life and that we must truly BREATHE. In the Bible, the act of bowing indicates one acknowledging God's kingship and showing reverence for His power.  When we are going through trials and tribulations, we often will feel powerless, and in some regards, we are. However, our true power is not in ourselves but rather in our reliance on God and our faith that He will extend His grace and mercy during our difficult season.

When my clients come to me for the grief of divorce, there are times when I deem disclosure therapeutically apropos. When they hear my story, they are amazed to see the woman sitting across them beaming with joy.  Oftentimes, they ask me, *"how did you make it?"* and my answer is, *"I remembered to BREATHE."* Prayer was and is the beginning of breathwork. Bowing before God is a necessary component of inhaling the peace of God and exhaling the pain.  Bowing before Him is not about the posture of your physical being but, rather, the posture of your heart.  God is concerned about the matters of our hearts, and when we pray, He hears us.

## REACH OUT FOR HELP

*Bear one another's burdens, and so fulfill the law of Christ.*

*Galatians 6:2 9 New King James Version*

One of the biggest mistakes I made at the beginning of my grief journey was not to ask for help. I had always been the friend or family member who seemingly had it all together and usually was the one, others would come to for answers. During this season of my life, I could barely help myself, and I certainly had no answers. I remember being so consumed with fear that it was paralyzing. There was so much I did not know about divorce or the grief process that simply navigating through the day evoked even more fear. If I am honest with myself, pride was the main reason I failed to initially ask for help. I was embarrassed that I had spoken so openly about the wonderful marriage that God had blessed me with. I was a school counselor and licensed therapist who should have understood why I felt that way.

I am so glad that I did not stay in this place of mental, emotional, and spiritual stagnation for too long because one way to get beyond where you are is to move. So, I moved out of my way and, in prayer, heard the instructions of God to reach out to others and be honest about what I needed. I needed a lot! I needed prayer. I needed a listening ear. I needed a good divorce attorney and to discover how to get custody of my kids and get child support. I needed to know what would happen to my house since my husband stopped helping with my mortgage, and I couldn't afford to pay it on my own. I needed a good therapist to help me navigate my feelings. I needed help with transporting my kids sometimes. There were times when I needed food or help with bills. Although it was hard to ask for things that I'd never had to ask others for, I knew that God had used me to help others during their times of need and trusted that He could do the same for me.  Looking back, I recognize that God not only ordered my steps during one of my life's most difficult moments but also ordered the steps of those to whom I reached out for help.

When we are in the midst of our breathwork, we must remember to extend our reach.  During prayer time, sit quietly and ask God to reveal who He wants you to reach out to and obey His instructions.  I promise you that there are people in your life who are not just willing to help but wanting and waiting to help you during your storm.

## ESTABLISH A LIFE STRATEGY

My life had changed drastically.  I realized that I could either shift my way of doing things, or I would be shifted into doing things.  I chose the former.  During the "reach" portion of my breathwork, I sought counsel from my friends who I knew were single moms and had limited help from their children's fathers. As I type this, I cringe at the fact that I am actually putting this down as a potential tool to use.  I believe it is extremely ridiculous and unfair that a parent with a living and breathing co-parent on the earth has to figure out how to take care of their children alone. But this was my new reality, and I had to strategize. One of my close friends, Katrina, told me I needed to learn to think like a single parent.  I was perplexed at what that would look like because I was never required to think from a single perspective since the onset of becoming a mother.  But this is what I did.  I learned how to be thankful when my son's dad decided to step up and help out, but I stopped expecting it. Doing this released me from expending unnecessary energy on getting angry when he failed to do something he said he would. And so, I developed a strategic system that helped me navigate my new normal.

One of the major changes that occurred during this time was my finances.  My pending divorce took a massive toll on me financially, and I couldn't even make ends meet.  As stated earlier, my sons were very active throughout the school year.  They had already endured so much pain that I wanted them to keep a semblance of normalcy when keeping them in their activities.  During football season, I knew I had to pay for my youngest son's games every Wednesday and for my eldest son's high school games every Friday.  The amount of money I would spend each week seems minuscule to me now. Still, during this time, it was a matter of using the money for the game or making sure my sons had lunch money for the following week! Thus, after praying for a strategy and reaching out to others for advice, one of the things I did was join the high school paint team.  I was informed that any parent who volunteered to help paint the football field before games could get into all of the home games for free! So, I volunteered for the paint team during the last two years of my eldest son's football career and during my youngest son's tenure as a high school football player.  Although I had to pay to get into away games, I would ride to the away games with other parents to save on gas money.  I must admit it was very tiring physically to paint the football field. Still, I had such a wonderful time getting to know the other parents and seeing the delight in my son's eyes when they saw me rush to the field to greet them. I was there for every football game they ever played in middle and high school!

When going through difficult moments, it may appear that small things are not as important as the major things we have to deal with.  Though I had to develop a strategy for the bigger changes I needed to make, seeing my sons play football was just as important to God as it was to me.

God knows what we are dealing with and the toll life's changes have on His children. As you think about establishing your life's strategy, remember that "God causes all things (even the simplest things like being able to fund attending a child's football game) to work together for the good of them who love him and are called according to His purpose." (Romans 8:28)

## ACCEPT YOUR LIMITATIONS

This part of my breathwork was difficult for me since I was so determined to be a super mom. I put on my imaginary cape and took on my world, forgetting that even Superman could not withstand kryptonite! I soon learned that the only thing heroically super about me was recognizing that God was my power and my strength. I will never forget how devastated I was to learn that my youngest son had been cut from the middle school basketball team for the second year in a row. I was so upset because he had worked so hard and had come so far in his journey, only to be disappointed. One of the life strategies I would establish at this time was figuring out how to help my son develop his basketball skills. I know this would require a performance coach that I could not afford.

I prayed about this situation and reached out to a friend whose son played basketball on an AAU team. She encouraged me to allow my son to come to try out for one of the teams she knew was developing a new team for his age group. My son was so excited to discover that he had impressed the coach enough that he was willing to work with him to help him develop. Being a part of the team meant that my son's bruised esteem would be mended somewhat. Thankfully, it also meant that I found a way to assist in his athletic development without paying an astronomical amount for a strength and conditioning coach. Although I enjoyed being a part of the AAU world, the first season became so taxing that I realized I had to do more breathwork and reconsider this part of my strategy. The team's practice was over 30 minutes from my home, and practice was several times per week. They also had several games every weekend at a gym that was a 45-minute drive from our house. My son had a great experience, and we finished the season victoriously. However, when it was time to decide how to proceed the following year, I had to make some adjustments. I no longer had the physical or financial ability to keep my son in AAU. Thankfully, he made the basketball team during 8th grade and understood when I told him he could no longer play on an AAU team.

Furthermore, my eldest son understood that I could not make it to all of his indoor and outdoor track meets but would definitely make it to most of them. I had to accept that as much as I wanted to be able to do everything that I simply could not. There is an amazing surge of strength that one discovers during their storms, but even the strongest winds have limits on what they can blow through. Once we acknowledge and accept the areas in which we are limited, we can re-establish our strategies and continue down our paths, ensuring that we breathe!

## THINK POSITIVELY

*Finally, brethren, whatsoever things are true, whatsoever things are honest, whatsoever things are just, whatsoever things are pure, whatsoever things are lovely, whatsoever things are of good report; if there be any virtue, and if there be any praise, think on these things.*

*Philippians 4:8 King James Version*

This may sound cliche, but positive thinking is essential when grieving the loss of a relationship. Although I was doing the necessary work to move forward with my life, that doesn't mean that this necessary work was not extremely difficult.  I often got so angry with my ex-husband when I would think about how difficult my life was compared to his!  I would ruminate on negativity so much that I would respond by sending him an ugly text message that was extremely rude or saying the vilest things. Although I felt better for a moment, I would get convicted and have to repent.  I hated doing this, and my ex-husband found it laughable that I thought this was "Godly" behavior *(whew chile, thank God for His grace and mercy because I was a piece of work)*.

As a therapist who leans towards a cognitive behavioral therapeutic framework, I understand that the way we think determines how we feel and how we feel determines what we do.  I often discuss the aspect of the vicious thought cycle with my clients. I teach them how to use specific strategies to combat these negative thoughts and cognitive distortions that cause them to be reactive and feel emotionally dysregulated.  I was very angry and had every right to be.  However, during my reaching out stage, I was told that I had to think like a single mom, and I also had to accept my limitations.  One of them being stinking thinking.  I started to utilize thought-stopping and cognitive reframing to minimize the effects of negativity and retrain my brain to think better.  When I started thinking better, I started feeling better and doing better.  Remember, the Bible says, *"as a man thinketh so is he" (Proverbs 23:7a)*.  Thus, it is important to keep track of what we allow our minds to focus on so we don't become that negative thing.  Lastly, we must remember that this is a season of transformation, and the only way to do this is to renew our minds *(Romans 12:2)*.

## *HEAL EMOTIONALLY*

One of my favorite biblical stories about healing is in Matthew chapter 15, verses 22 through 30.  This story is of a woman who, by custom, should not have come to Jesus to request healing. Yet, she did so anyway, exercising her faith in His healing ability as well as His extension of grace.  This is the story where we hear the quote, "healing is the children's bread," being referenced.  In this story, Jesus teaches us that He is a God who heals us based on who He is as opposed to who we are. It teaches us that healing is our basic right as children of God.

Although we, as believers, have a cerebral knowledge that we have a right to be healed, I've noticed in my practice that many believers lack that experiential knowledge of the healing of Christ.  As I assessed why some believers believe in the power of God to heal while not receiving it, I discovered that many of these people have a hard time accepting the healing of God because of low self-worth.  One of the enemy's tactics is to highlight our trials in a way that we begin to ponder if we are being punished and forsaken by God.

When I was dealing with the death of my father while at the same time feeling devastated by the death of my marriage, I fell prey to doing all I could to take care of my sons while neglecting to take care of myself.  I am so glad that during prayer, God instructed me to reach out to help and showed me the people positioned to walk me toward my healing.  My healing was a process that honestly took a few years and is something I continue to manage.  Although I believe that deliverance can take place instantaneously, I see the management of that deliverance as a process of healing.  In my clinical opinion, healing indicates that a person no longer negatively responds to triggers that remind them of their past traumatic experiences. Furthermore, they see through the lens of expectation as opposed to the lens of their experiences.

When doing breathwork, we must think positively and meditate on scriptures relevant to what we are enduring. For example, the woman in the above story wasn't worried about Jewish customs when it came to her need for healing. Just like this woman, we need to move past the situation we are enduring and trust that we deserve healing too! I knew I was enduring an intensely traumatic time in my life and trusted that emotional healing was the bread I needed to nourish my soul.

## EMBRACE YOUR NEW NORMAL

The last part of the breathwork I did was to embrace my new normal. I spent so many years looking back at all that I had lost that I could not clearly focus on all that I had gained! Go back and read that sentence again. How ironic was it that there was also gain during a period of loss?

The biblical story that comes to mind as I ponder the scriptural reference for this part is that of Lot's wife. In Genesis 19:15-26, God tells Lot to take his wife and daughters out of the city of Sodom to escape its demise. In verse 26, Lot's wife looks back to view the city now in flames and is turned into a pillar of salt. In the New Testament, Jesus warns His disciples about looking back in Luke 17:32, saying, "Remember Lot's wife!" I thank God for His mercy because I surely would have literally been the "salt of the earth" during the early years of my grief. I looked back at how much had changed during the holidays. We had so many family traditions that I truly enjoyed and no longer could experience. I looked back on how easier my life was when I had another adult living with me and helping me pay bills and take care of our kids. I looked back at how much my parents did for the boys and me and how I didn't even have my dad during the worst season of my life. I looked back so long that I almost tripped over the extraordinary life that was right in front of me. Looking back not only reminded me of what I had lost, but it also reminded me of the excruciating pain that I had endured. Every glimpse in the rearview mirror was connected with a negative thought, and that thought was connected to a negative feeling. I had to not only think positively and heal emotionally, but I also had to embrace my new normal.

When I think of an embrace, I think of something comforting and worth holding on to. It may not feel like you are living a life worth embracing, but it is! Jesus promises us abundant life, and this promise is not contingent on us never experiencing death or divorce. God wants us to expect His abundance. So, doing breathwork, I had to get in front of my grief and establish a strategy to accept what I lost and embrace what I gained. I am still as passionate about holidays today as I was before, probably even more so. I now have new holiday traditions that transcend spending it with only one family but, sometimes, with a host of many families! I enjoy every moment I have with my mom, siblings, and sons because I know that tomorrow is not promised. I want to soak in all of the time with them like a sponge, ready to ring out the water of joy.

I have embraced the fact that our pain pushed my sons and me closer than we have ever been and that we all have developed unique talents as a result of our pain. I now have a private practice operating in two states, and books and products coming out soon. My eldest son is a college graduate and professional writer by career and is pursuing his passion for music. My youngest son is working on his degree and is currently developing his passion for directing and producing.

God has been so gracious to my sons and me. We all honestly realize that our pain produced our purpose. It may be tempting to look back at your past life in flames, but the Sodom of your life is burning for a reason. Do not look back! Keep your eyes on God and move ahead with purpose!

## Plan & Think

*Don't copy the behavior and customs of this world,
but let God transform you into a new person
by changing the way you think.
Then you will learn to know God's will for you,
which is good and pleasing and perfect.*

*Romans 12:2 New Living Translation*

As previously mentioned, I tend to theoretically adhere to a cognitive behavioral framework. Although I believe our cognitions impact how we think, which affects what we do, I am not admonishing you to pretend that everything is gumdrops and lollipops. But I am certainly telling you to be cognizant of how you think and be aware of any automatic negative thoughts, faulty cognitions, or negative core beliefs you may have adopted during a painful or traumatic season. As a result, I have developed "Quik 5 W's" (questions to ponder when making a quick decision in a crisis) that helped countless clients gain control over their cognitive distortions and create healthier thought patterns that ultimately help them set specific goals.

### Quick 5 W's
1. What Do I Need Now?
2. What Do I Want Later?
3. What Do I Know?  What Don't I Know?
4. What Do I Have?  What Don't I Have?
5. What Can I Do Now?

The Quick 5 W's can be used to help you sort through a myriad of issues. Here is an example of what I did for one of my major issues early on in my grief process.

*My Quick 5 W's for Finances:*
1. *I need to make more money to offset the money I no longer get from my ex-husband.*
2. *I want to be able to take care of my sons, pay all my bills,*

*and have the ability to save and invest in our future.*
*I want to be able to do this on my own income.*
3.   *I do not know how this will work out, but I do know that God knows!*
4.   *I have an LPC.  I have the ability to get a second job or find one that makes more money.  I have my faith in God. I don't have a consistent co-parent helping me with the boys.  I don't have a lot of flexibility because of the boys' schedules,*
5.   *I can look for part-time work and talk to my friends who are in private practice to see if they need any help in their practices.*

This seems basic, but it helped me get all these thoughts out of my head and onto paper.  It also helped me be specific when reaching out to people to ask for the help I needed.

## Pray

*⁶ Don't worry about anything; instead, pray about everything.*
*Tell God what you need and thank him for all he has done.*
*⁷ Then you will experience God's peace,*
*which exceeds anything we can understand.*
*His peace will guard your hearts and minds as you live in Christ Jesus.*

*Philippians 4:6-7 New Living Translation*

1. **PREPARE MY HEART**
   a. to feel
   b. to heal
   c. to let go
   d. to recover

2. **PREPARE MY MIND**
   a. To fight (negative thoughts)
   b. To forgive
   c. To focus
   d. To renew

3. **POSITION ME TO PURSUE**
   a. Purpose I'm called to
   b. People I'm supposed to be connected to
   c. Places I'm to travel too
   d. Power to execute the plan

# CONCLUSION

I used to fear that people would deem me irresponsible for liking divorce with that of death. Yet, since I have experienced both the death of a parent and the death of a marriage, I am aware of the truths that lie beneath the notion that divorce is akin to death! Yes, you have experienced an unexpected death! The death of your Happily Ever After until death do you part! You may experience all the stages of grief, as did I, or you may not have had the opportunity to grieve appropriately. Despite where you may fall in this category, it is imperative that you make sure that you are communicating with yourself to do so without fear.

As I ponder the notion of death being akin to divorce, I think about the many clients I have counseled while enduring the various stages of grief. For example, I remember a client who lost their spouse of over twenty years due to a tragedy. Though the client was still a healthy and viable individual, she might as well have given herself over to death because she remained stuck in the part of grief that prevented her from moving on! She simply could not get past the idea that she would have to live the rest of her life without her best friend of 20-something years and certainly did not think she could do so and actually be happy! By the same token, I have walked alongside women who have suffered the devastating blows of divorce. They soon realized that their fixation on what they thought they had, and would always have, made it extremely difficult for them to move forward without their ex-spouses. Thus, they remained stuck!

What causes a woman to get stuck anyway? There is a conglomerate of good answers, but my favorite answer is HER THOUGHTS! Even the Bible teaches us about the importance of our thoughts.

*For as he thinketh in his heart, so is he:*

*Proverbs 23:7a King James Version*

***As a man thinketh so IS HE!*** I believe women get stuck in the vicious thought cycle of what was supposed to be versus what will never be. So many women fight for dear life to have yet another unresolved issue to cling to. For a least then, she will have something, even if it is a painful something!

In my counseling practice, my clients often ask me how I stopped loving the man I once was infatuated with and loved immensely. My short answer is I allowed myself to look at my ex-husband through what I call "a corrective lens of truth"! I used to look at our relationship through my blurred vision of what I thought we had and what I saw us having one day. My sight was severely out of focus as I looked at my ex-husband through the lens of bitterness and disdain. I had a right to be angry, and I had a right to show my contempt. But the Word of God tells us that everything that is permissible is not beneficial. (1 Cor 10:23). Looking at my situation through this lens dimmed my vision in all areas. I had become a very negative and pessimistic person and focused on what I saw as reality. However, 2 Corinthians 4:17 admonishes us not to look at what we can see because what we see is temporary. My false reality made me peer through a lens where the negative would last forever. But God's eyes see through eternity! So I decided to correct my lens by gazing at the Word of God until I saw it as the truth.

The corrective lens deemed that a husband is to love his wife like Christ loved the church so much that he gave himself for it (Eph 5:25).  The corrective lens of my truth was that I was in love with someone who did not treat me the way that God said I deserve to be treated.  When I was finally able to preview the life I was supposed to have by reading the Word, I began seeing what I "truly" had and stopped looking at what I "truly" wanted. It was then the eros feelings of love I once had for my husband dissipated.  With the corrected lens of Christ, I worked on seeing my ex-spouse via the eyes of Christ and began loving him with the agape kind of love.

More importantly, I learned to love myself and appreciate my new life.  Now, I am happy, I have joy, and I have peace. I still have a fighting spirit and often must get back in the ring to defend my title, but I have the best trainer in the world! He is developing me into a fighter that will never lose!  **TKO!**

# ABOUT THE AUTHOR

Daniall Marshall Foskey is recognized as a "Three Best Rated Marriage Counselor," often referred to as a "Soul-Digger." Ms. Foskey is a therapeutic genius, excavating coals from souls and making them diamonds. She helps clients identify soul wounds and uses her clinical expertise and affirmative words as an ointment to heal soul infections. Clients often leave with their identities revived, futures reimagined, and confidence rekindled.

A native of Jacksonville, North Carolina, Ms. Foskey grew up as one of three children and spent her time learning to fully embrace the purpose-driven person that her parents raised her to be! Having experienced divorce, the loss of her father and material possessions, Daniall knows firsthand the impact of trauma, which makes her qualified, both professionally and personally, to connect with those who have found themselves struck out by life curveballs. She has taken those curve balls and knocked them out of the park to run back home to the base of her soul.

As a former Chesapeake Public Schools Guidance Counselor of 13 years, Ms. Foskey has witnessed the systemic effects of unresolved familial grief and trauma on students' overall academic and psychosocial prowess. As a result of her experiences and observations in the school system, she sought to build her private practice. Daniall is a former co-owner of

Psychological Associates of Greater Hampton Roads (PAGHR), which was a pillar in the Portsmouth, Virginia, area, providing effective therapy for children, adolescents, individuals, couples, and groups.

She is now the CEO of Daniall Marshall Foskey & Associates, a private practice in Portsmouth, VA, with a new location in Charlotte, North Carolina. She is also launching a series of SOUL-Workshops entitled, *Her EPISOUL.* It was created to help women move past the episodic pain from their life and utilize all that they have to fuel purpose! A graduate of The University of NC at Greensboro, Daniall holds a Bachelor of Science in Exercise and Sports Science. She also has a Master of Science in Community Counseling and School Counseling from Regent University. Ms. Foskey is a certified Aerobics instructor and personal trainer with over 15 years of experience.

During Daniall's downtime, you may find this self-proclaimed "HolyQT" writing, speaking, ministering, or even teaching a Zumba class! She is a die-hard Dallas Cowboys fan and a proud mom to Jaylen, a Virginia Tech alumnus, and Jai, a Junior at North Carolina A & T State University.